Classic Solo Piano Arrangements by Fred Bock
with optional transitions by Dick Bolks

Three Favorites of Bill & Gloria Gaither

for solo piano

table of contents

GET ALL EXCITED

WILLIAM J. GAITHER
Arranged by FRED BOCK

17
a little louder
21
25
29
cresc. poco a poco
33
Strong
ff

37
41
45
f cresc.
49
ff
53
8va
Optional Segue
f
mf molto rit.
mp

GENTLE SHEPHERD

WILLIAM J. and GLORIA GAITHER
Arranged by FRED BOCK

17
21
mf
ten.
ten.
25
29
33

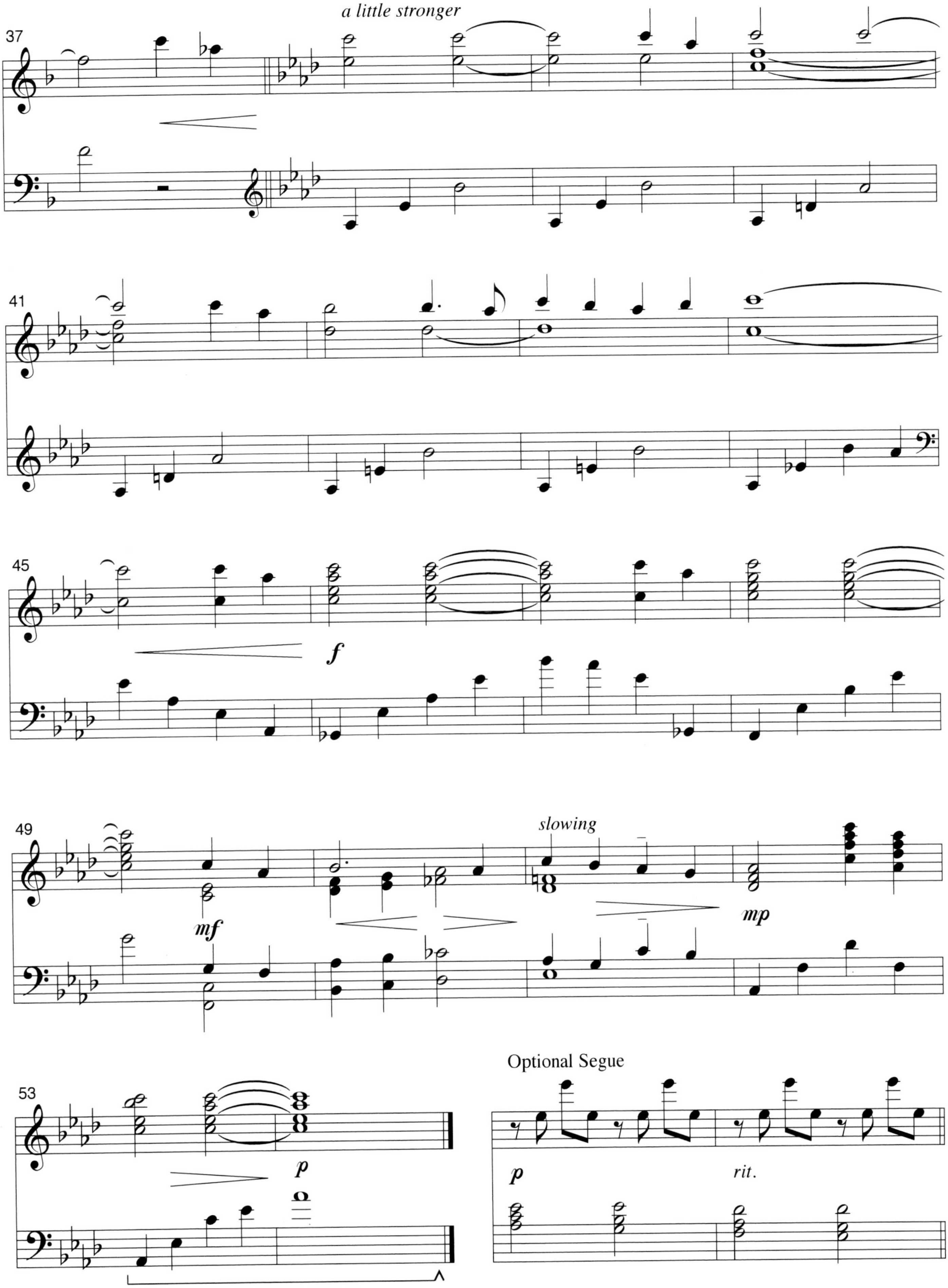
a little stronger
37
41
45
f
49
slowing
mf
mp
53
p
Optional Segue
p
rit.

THE KING IS COMING

WILLIAM J. GAITHER
Arranged by FRED BOCK

19
a little faster
24
29
34
a little faster
f
38
8vb
8vb
8vb

43
48
53
58
63
8vb
3
12

Brightly, with a strong gospel feel
67
ff
71
75
79
83
rit.
8va
8va
8va
8vb